Finn and the Salmon of Knowledge: mythology, toponymy and cosmology

Anthony Murphy

Published by Anthony Murphy, 80 Cedarfield,
Donore Road, Drogheda, Co. Louth, Ireland.
Email: mythicalireland@gmail.com
Website: www.mythicalireland.com

Text and images copyright © Anthony Murphy
First published 2021
Printed by Anglo Printers, Drogheda

ISBN 978-1-9993500-2-4

Other books by the author
Non-fiction:
Island of the Setting Sun: In Search of Ireland's Ancient Astronomers
(with Richard Moore), Liffey Press, 2006/2008/2020
Newgrange: Monument to Immortality, Liffey Press, 2012
The Mythology of Venus – Ancient Calendars and Archaeoastronomy
(collaborative, edited by Helen Benigni), University Press of America,
2013
Mythical Ireland: New Light on the Ancient Past, Liffey Press, 2017
Dronehenge: The Story Behind the Remarkable Discovery at Newgrange,
Liffey Press, 2019

Fiction:
Land of the Ever-Living Ones, 2013
The Cry of the Sebac, 2016
Return to Segais, 2021

Dedicated to all the scholars, past and present, whose diligent work shines a light upon ancient mysteries

Finn and the Salmon of Knowledge

Ar bá baile fallsigthe éicsi do grés lasna filedu for brú usci.

'For the poets thought that the place where poetry was revealed always was upon the brink of water'.[1]

Many people in Ireland know the story of the Salmon of Knowledge. Even if you've never heard any of our other myths, you are likely to have encountered the tale of how the young boy Fionn Mac Cumhaill (sometimes rendered Finn McCool) gained bardic insight and mystical illumination when he burnt his thumb on the Salmon of Knowledge (*Bradán Feasa*) which had been caught by Finnéces, a poet or seer, at the river Boyne near Brú na Bóinne.

We were told the story in school. It had special resonance for Drogheda schoolchildren because the Salmon of Knowledge was believed to have been caught at Fiacc's Pool, which is said to be located at Brú na Bóinne between Rosnaree and Knowth. So the story was set just five or six miles from the classrooms where we heard it as children.

There are many aspects of the tale, its location, the characters involved and associations with other deities and landscapes that make it a fascinating study for anyone interested in mythology and its relationship to folklore, philology, onomastics, toponymy and cosmology.

The story

The story of how Fionn/Finn/Find came to eat the salmon is contained in a Late Middle Irish narrative describing the boy's exploits and fortunes. The narrative, *Macgnímartha Find*, translates as 'The boyhood deeds of Finn', and is contained in a manuscript in the Bodleian Library at Oxford.[2]

This manuscript dates from the mid-15th century, but the story in its earliest written has been dated by Celtic scholar Kuno Meyer to the 12th century.[3] It is mostly composed of prose but there is some verse too.

Independent of the manuscript version of the story of the Salmon of Knowledge, a considerable number of modern folk renditions of the tale are known and have been seemingly propagated for centuries.[4]

The story about Finn and the Salmon of Knowledge, as related in the Bodleian Codex Laud 610, is a surprisingly concise one, and you might wonder where the lengthier dramatized oral versions come from. This laconic version is the sole manuscript copy of the tale:

> Seven years Finnéces had been on the Boyne, watching the salmon of Fec's Pool; for it had been prophesied of him that he would eat the salmon of Féc, when nothing would remain unknown to him. The salmon was found, and Demne was then ordered to cook the salmon; and the poet told him not to eat anything of the salmon. The youth brought him the salmon after cooking it. 'Hast thou eaten anything of the salmon, my lad?' says the poet. 'No,' says the youth, 'but I burned my thumb, and put it into my

mouth afterwards.' 'What is thy name, my lad?' says
he. 'Demne,' says the youth. 'Finn is thy name, my lad,'
says he; 'and to thee was the salmon given to be eaten,
and verily thou art the Finn.' Thereupon the youth
eats the salmon. It is that which gave the knowledge
to Finn, to wit, whenever he put his thumb into his
mouth, and sang through *teinm láida,* then whatever
he had been ignorant of would be revealed to him.
He learnt the three things that constitute a poet,
to wit, *teinm láida* and *imbas forosna,* and *dichetul
dichennaib.*[5]

    After burning his thumb on the salmon and putting
it into his mouth, thereby gaining all the wisdom of
the magic fish, Finn recited a lay to prove his sudden
endowment with poetic skill and talent.[6]

The meaning of the name Demne

It is most interesting that when asked his name, the boy said he was called 'Demne', but upon tasting the salmon he is told by Finnéces that he is now called Finn. Finnéces is described by scholars as a druid or seer but we know precious little about him. His name is from *finn* (fair, bright, white, lustrous, light-hued) and *éices* (seer, scholar, sage, poet), so that his title could be rendered 'Finn the seer'.[7] The white colour of the *finn* part of his name is 'strongly associated with the priestly, sacred class in many Indo-European traditions and is associated with druids' and *filid's* names in Irish material…'[8]

While it is clear that Finnéces permanently bestows the new name 'Finn' on the boy, the youth's previous name, Demne, is his birth name, something established earlier in the text of *Macgnímartha Find*:

> Cumall left his wife Muirne pregnant. And she brings forth a son, to whom the name of Demne was given.[9]

But just to add to the confusion about the boy's name, in an episode that occurs prior to his meeting with Finnéces by the Boyne, the boy Demne plays hurling and running with a group of youths at a stronghold in Moy Liffey.[10]

Demne's exploits on the playing field are nothing less than miraculous. First he beats one-quarter of the youths, then one-third, and finally when they all come against him, he wins the game 'from them all'.[11]

'What is thy name?' they said. 'Demne,' said he. The youths tell that to the man of the stronghold. 'Then kill him, if ye know how to do it — if ye are able to do it,' said he. 'We should not be able to do aught to him,' said they. 'Did he tell you his name?' says he. 'He said,' say they, 'that his name was Demne.' 'What does he look like?' said he. 'A shapely fair (*finn*) youth,' said they. 'Then Demne shall be named Finn, (the Fair),' said he. Whence the youths used to call him Finn.[12]

Curiously, he retains the name Finn from this episode (paragraph 9 of Macgnímartha Find) until he meets Finnéces (paragraph 18), at which point he reverts to using his birth name again. But from the moment Finnéces announces 'Finn is thy name, my lad' in the Salmon of Féc (Salmon of Knowledge) episode, the name Demne does not appear again.

There are indications here, perhaps, of initiation rituals (a sporting contest against more experienced players, and the eating of a magic fish) that might resonate with the boyhood deeds of another great hero of Irish myth, Sétanta/Cúchulainn, but before we come to that an exploration of the meaning of the name Demne is important.

Demne (rendered *deimhne* in modern Irish, and spelt a dozen different ways in medieval manuscripts) means 'firmness, stability, certainty, assurance',[13] and 'genuine, trustworthy, real, reliable'.[14]

One imagines that the certainty around Demne/Finn is the sureness that this boy is to become a very special and greatly renowned leader, possessor of arcane knowledge and warrior. Explicit in the tale of how he comes to eat the Salmon of Knowledge is that it is his fate to consume the magical fish, a fate which does not exasperate or frustrate Finnéces but rather consigns him to gentle resignation in the presence of the boy wonder.

'…verily thou art the Finn', Finnéces tells him. Why does he refer to him as 'the' Finn, meaning THE 'bright/lustrous/fair' one? Is it because he (the boy) is the one whose destiny it is to become the sacred possessor of divine, poetic or esoteric knowledge? In a remarkable role reversal, a short time after he eats the salmon at Linn Féic, Finn takes the name of his druid master/initiator: 'At that time the name of Cumall's son was Finnéces',[15] and thus the boy Finn becomes 'Finn the seer'.[16]

Another variant of Finn's boyhood name is Demne Máel (Deimne Maol in modern Irish). 'Demne implies assurance or firmness and stability. Máel denotes short hair, and associations with druidism and the Otherworld.'[17]

In the Irish text of the salmon story in *Macgnímartha Find*, the boy is referred to as '*in gilla*', meaning the boy, the youth, or the attendant or gillie, man-servant or messenger.[18] But a *gilla* can also mean 'a youth of an age to bear arms'.[19]

As a servant or assistant to Finnéces (Finn the Seer), the boy Demne is given specific instructions to cook the salmon for his master, but these instructions are accompanied by a conspicuous proscription: '…and the poet told him not to eat anything of the salmon'.[20] However, when the boy accidentally burns his thumb on the holy fish and then instinctively places his thumb in his mouth to numb the pain, the proscription is dissolved and the blameless youth inherits the arcane enlightenment of the sacred salmon.

There are overt connotations in the story of the Salmon of Féc of an initiation of the boy Finn, and one can see in the tale suggestions of rites of passage in which Finn's social or religious status changes dramatically. The famous American professor of literature and comparative mythology and religion Joseph Campbell might have referred to Finnéces's role in Finn's story as 'supernatural aid'. In a chapter of that title in *The Hero With a Thousand Faces,* Campbell tells us:

> 'For those who have not refused the call [to adventure], the first encounter of the hero-journey is with a protective figure (often a little old crone or old man) who provides the adventurer with amulets against the dragon forces he is about to pass.'[21]

Campbell further tells us that 'what such a figure represents is the benign, protecting power of destiny'[22] and indeed destiny has a significant role in the Salmon of Knowledge episode. Campbell adds that 'though omnipotence may seem to be endangered by the threshold passages and life awakenings, protective power is always and ever present within the sanctuary of the heart and even immanent within, or just behind, the unfamiliar features of the world. One has only to know and trust, and the ageless guardians will appear'.[23]

Not infrequently, Campbell reminds us, the supernatural helper is masculine in form.[24]

The tale Macgnímartha Find (which translates more literally as the doings or acts (*gníomh*) of the boy (*mac*)

Finn (Find)) is, in fact, something akin to a chronicle of his initiation from boy to man, from innocent lad to fearsome warrior, and of the "dragon forces" in the form of the sons of Morna who have been pursuing him or lying in wait for him since his birth.[25] The story is similar in some regards to the *'Macgnímrada'* or Boyhood Deeds of Cúchulainn,[26] who gains his infamous name when he miraculously kills the giant blood hound of the Ulster smith, Culann.[27] As a boy, he is known as Sétanta,[28] but gains his 'adult' name Cúchulainn at the age of seven when, having slain the giant hound, he offers to take the place of the dead dog until he can rear a whelp to take the deceased animal's place as guardian of Culann and his cattle – whence *Cú-Chulainn*, the Hound of Culann.[29] Like Finn, Sétanta also excels on the playing field, where 'thrice fifty' youths throw javelins, balls and hurling-clubs at the boy but he wards them all off so that none touches him.[30] 'Like Cúchulainn, Finn captures two wild stags, and on another occasion he brings home a live duck after shooting it.'[31]

Where is Fiacc's Pool?

The location and even the name of the pool where the Salmon of Knowledge is caught is significant to the theme of initiation in Finn's story. However, Macgnímartha Find does not specify the location, other than to tell us it is 'on the Boyne'.[32] For a more specific location, we have to refer to other sources. The single best reference book in which to find all the instances of the Irish names of places, personages and tribes in medieval manuscripts is Edmund Hogan's exhaustive (one might even correctly say 'epic') *Onomasicon Goedelicum.*[33] I am lucky enough to possess a printed copy, but thanks to the dedicated work of scholars a digital version is available online in a searchable PDF format.[34]

Hogan tells us that Linn Féic (Féic's Pool or Fiacc's Pool) is near the townland of Rossnaree in the parish of Knockcommon, barony of Lower Duleek, county Meath.[35] Thankfully, the locale of Linn Féic is generally known although the precise location is not pinpointed. Folio 196b of the Book of Lismore tells us that Linn Féic is near Cleitech,[36] and thanks to the diligence of another scholar, Elizabeth Hickey, the location of Cleitech is now fairly well attested.[37] A mound associated with the deity Elcmar, who was deposed from Síd in Broga (Newgrange),[38] and later with Derg of Swift Eloquence, was located at Cleitech.[39]

The Metrical Dindshenchas poem about Brug na Bóinde (poem I) composed by Cináed ua Hartacán (who died in the 10th century) tells us:

Atchíu lind find Féic na Fían
frit aniar, ní timm in gním.

I see the clear pool of Fiacc of the warriors
west of thee, —not feeble the deed—[40]

We know Fiacc's pool is on the western extremity of
Brú na Bóinne, whose limits are not easily extrapolated
from the manuscripts, but whose extent is, approximately
speaking, in the vicinity of the great bend of the Boyne
encompassing the giant mounds of Newgrange (called
Tech mic ind Óc by ua Hartacán), Knowth (Cnogba)
and Dowth (Dubad), along with many other smaller
monuments. Given that Newgrange is the first of the
places of eminence described in the poem, and Fiacc's
pool is listed next, we can surmise that Fiacc's pool was
an important feature of the complex. It is also obvious
from the foregoing that Linn Féic is roughly west of
Newgrange. In fact, Fiacc's pool being adjacent to or close
to Cleitech (which Hickey identified as the place now
occupied by Rosnaree House), it is obvious that Fiacc's
pool lies somewhere in the stretch of river between the
old ford of Rosnaree and Broe weir between Rosnaree
and Knowth – the latter was constructed to deepen the
Boyne as part of the Boyne Navigation[41] in the second
half of the 18th century.[42] (See *Figure 1*, p. 16)
   There are two old weirs in this stretch of the river
which were 'built on or in close proximity to the medieval
fish weir of Rosnaree which belonged to the Cistercian
abbey of Mellifont'.[43] Arthur Went says that these weirs
are 'with the exception of certain details … virtually the

same as those erected and maintained by the monks of Mellifont for nearly four centuries'.[44]

If you've ever seen salmon jumping over a weir in the Boyne you'll know what an extraordinary sight it is. Atlantic salmon (*Salmo salar*) spawned in pools in the upper reaches of the Boyne make their way past Rosnaree/Linn Féic and eventually find their way out to the Irish Sea and on into the northern Atlantic Ocean. These same fish (and this is a remarkable fact about all Atlantic salmon) eventually find their way back to not just their natal river, but with remarkable precision to the same location where they hatched, in order to spawn the next generation of salmon.[45]

A salmon angler intimately familiar with this area of the river tells me that salmon will often 'rest up' in the deeper water behind these weirs at Rosnaree in the summer before continuing their journey upriver later. These may be the grilse, salmon who return to the Boyne in July having spent just one winter at sea. Salmon fishermen will relate that jumping over weirs can tax a fish to the point of exhaustion, and it makes sense then that the salmon will rest in the deeper, stiller water beyond the weir.

The two weirs at Rosnaree certainly look ancient, although admittedly I have absolutely no knowledge of the dating of salmon weirs or the materials used in their construction. However, in comparison to, say, the large weir at the bridge over the Boyne in Slane with its neat, straight edge, the Rosnaree pair look strangely rugged or even serpentine as they stretch sinuously across almost the whole width of the river diagonally.

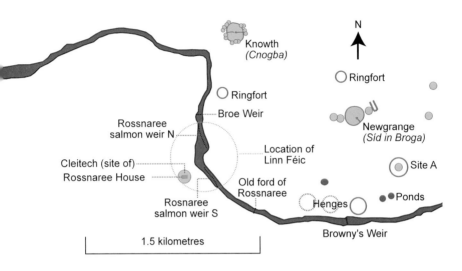

Figure 1: Location of Fiacc's Pool, Rossnaree weirs, Cleitech and some of the major monuments at Brú na Bóinne.

Figure 2: An aerial view of the southern of the two salmon weirs at Rossnaree.

Figure 3: An annotated aerial view (looking northwest) showing the Rossnaree salmon weirs, Rossnaree House (the location of Síd Cleitech) and Broe Weir.

Figure 4: The Mill House at Rossnaree and the location of the old ford of Rossnaree. Photos by the author.

The earliest written version of Macgnímartha Find goes back to the 12th century, which is the century in which the Cistercians arrived, built Mellifont Abbey, took control of large tracts of farmland in the area (including land at Newgrange) and built weirs and traps for fishing on the river Boyne.[46] It may be the case that salmon weirs were constructed in tidal rivers such as the Boyne before the Middle Ages, but there is scant information about whether stone weirs might have been built more anciently. Nonetheless, it seems quite certain that Fiacc's Pool was located in the vicinity of the old weirs at Rosnaree. One of the weirs listed as being in the possession of Mellifont Abbey at the time of its dissolution in the 16th century had a pool (*stagnus aque*) associated with it.[47] The weir was called 'Monknetone Were' (sic., read 'Monknewtown Weir') which was actually at Rosnaree,[48] not in the townland of Monknewtown which is about 2km to the north of Rosnaree and at a distance from the Boyne. Is this pool (*stagnus aque*) the same as Fiacc's pool, a place, perhaps, where the salmon rested after jumping one of the weirs there?

The location of another weir named 'Browny's Were' is disputed. Geraldine Stout places it at Rosnaree (the southern of the two weirs there),[49] while Went says that Westropp equated Browny to Brugh near Newgrange and placed it further east.[50] Given that Broe weir, Broe lock and Broe House in the vicinity are all possible Anglicisations or distortions of the old word 'Brug',[51] is it possible that Browny is another corruption of same? (I'm thinking in particular of Brú na Bóinne, hence a corruption might yield something like 'Browny Boyne'.[52])

The meaning of Linn Féic

The meaning of the name Fiacc's pool (Féc's pool, Féic's pool) is not entirely clear, although it seems it might have been named after one Fiac/Féic who drowned there.[53] It is probable that this is the same 'Fiacc of the warriors' mentioned in ua Hartacán's poem in the Metrical Dindshenchas.[54] Fiacc was a widely used name in early Ireland, and may have been a diminutive of the names Fiachra and Fiachu.[55]

But there are other possible extrapolations of the meaning of Féic's pool. One possibility is derived from the early 10th century *Sanas Chormaic*, popularly known as Cormac's Glossary, a dictionary of over 1,400 words compiled by Cormac úa Cuilennáin, a king-bishop of Cashel.[56]

There is of course the modern Irish *féach*, meaning to look, see or behold,[57] but although this can be rendered as *féig* in earlier Irish forms,[58] it does not appear as *féic* in any manuscript. The idea of Linn Féic being some sort of 'looking pool' or 'seeing pool' where one might seek out one's destiny seems romantic, but is not supported by the linguistic evidence.

Looking up the Irish word *féic* in the Electronic Dictionary of the Irish Language (eDIL) online,[59] the meaning is given as 'a ridge-pole, roof-tree, also the top or roof of a house'; also 'a top, summit, fig. highest point, acme'.[60] But that doesn't make any sense whatsoever in the context of a pool of water in a river. Could there be another meaning of the word?

Cormac's Glossary does have the word *feici*, which O'Donovan translates as 'ridgepole',[61] but the entry also adds '*quasi feighe* ['illumination'] *iarsindi imfuilnges soillsi dond tegh* ('because it sustains light for the house').[62] Finding this *feighe* in Sanas Chormaic, I decided to see if the word was in the Electronic Dictionary of the Irish Language. The latter does have the word *féig*, which is translated as 'of sight, seeing, keen-sighted', and 'of objects of sight, clear, luminous' and 'of mental and moral qualities, etc, keen, penetrating, acute'.[63] Could Linn Féic mean something like the 'pool of keen sight'?

At least one of the modern folk renditions of the story of the Salmon of Knowledge refers to the place where Fionn caught it as 'Feg's pool'.[64]

Other mentions of Linn Féic are made in *Agallam na Seanórach*, 'Colloquy of the Ancients', where it is described as 'the Pool of Fiacc on the bright-flowing Boyne'.[65]

An alternative name for Linn Féic might have been Linn Rois, mention of which is made in the Annals of the Four Masters and the Annals of Ulster for the year 841, and the Annals of Clonmacnoise for the year 839:

> A fleet of Norsemen on the Boinn, at Linn-Rois.[66]
> A fleet of Norsemen on the Boyne, at Linn-Rois.[67]
> There was a fleet of Normans at Lynnrosa upon the river of Boyne...[68]

O'Donovan tells us in his notes to Annals of the Four Masters that Linn-Rois is 'the Pool of Ros. This was the name of that part of the River Boyne opposite Rosnaree, in the barony of Lower Duleek, and county of Meath'.[69] But he does not tell us who or what Ros/Rois might be.

Figure 5: Aerial view of the area of the Boyne where Linn Féic/Linn Rois was located. Photo by the author.

The name of the townland of Rosnaree[70] is supposedly derived from Ros na Ríogh, meaning 'wood of the Kings'.[71] It is likely that the 'kings' referred to in the name of Rosnaree were the illustrious Cormac mac Airt, king of Ireland at Tara, who retired and died at Cleitech,[72] and Muirchertach Mac Erca, who is said to have dwelt at the house of Cleitech in the 6th century AD.[73]

A question arises about Linn-Rois. Is it the Pool of Ros, Ros being an abbreviation of Ros na Ríogh/ Rosnaree, or does it mean something else? The Irish word *ros* can also mean a headland or a promontory,[74] which might be somewhat apt for the foreland of Rosnaree upon which Cleitech was located with its fantastic, expansive views over the river valley below, but is hardly appropriate for a deep part of the river Boyne. Cormac's Glossary suggests that *ross* may refer to still water, being derived from *rofhoss*, meaning 'great rest', for 'it never is save on stagnant water'.[75] This is certainly a possibility for Linn Rois, especially if it was a deep pool just upstream of a salmon weir where the water might have been still ('stagnus aque').[76]

However, one more fascinating possibility presents itself. According to the Electronic Dictionary of the Irish Language, *ros* is also a poetic and cryptic word meaning 'knowledge',[77] possibly derived from the compound *ro-fis*,[78] *ro* denoting the possession of a quality in a high degree,[79] and *fis* meaning 'knowledge' or the acquisition of knowledge.[80] Does Linn Rois mean 'Pool of Knowledge' or 'Pool of Great Knowledge'? This certainly resonates with the notion of catching the *Eo Feasa*, the Salmon of Knowledge, in its waters.

Later, we will examine some deities and their links with the salmon of Linn Féic, one of whom has distinct nomenclature related to knowledge.

Demne's revelation

The boy Demne is endowed with significant talents or skills as a result of consuming the magic fish:

> He learnt the three things that constitute a poet: to wit, *teinm láida,* and *imbas forosna,* and *dichetul dichennaib.*[81]

The three in the Irish are rendered *teínm laega, imus forosna,* and *dicedul dicennaib* in the manuscript.[82] But what are these mysterious new abilities gained by the youth, who is now referred to by Finnéces as 'the Finn'?

The earliest attestations of these three poetic skills are contained in the 10th century *Sanas Chormaic,* which we will come to shortly. Meyer translates *teinm láida* as 'illumination (?) of song'.[83] The narrative of the story gives us more detail: 'It is that which gave the knowledge to Finn, to wit, whenever he put his thumb into this mouth, and sang through *teinm láida,* then whatever he had been ignorant of would be revealed to him.'[84] He need only suck on his thumb to gain keen insight into something about which he was previously uninformed. Here, perhaps, we see the wise seer Finn revert to his innocent, infantile state – the baby sucking its thumb – in which condition of purity or non-corruption the truth is perhaps best revealed.

eDIL tells us that *teinm laída* (the fada in this case is on the i, not the a as in Meyer's transcript) is 'a divinatory incantation used by the filid'.[85] *Teinm* is related to *teinnid,* a verb meaning 'cuts, cracks, breaks'.[86] Gwynn suggests *teinm láida* means 'the cracking of a nut (i.e. the solving of a riddle) by means of a *láid* or song'.[87] Perhaps we can best summarise *teinm láida* as a revelation that 'breaks through' from some unknown source while reciting a special incantation or invocation.

The nuts which fell from the magic hazel trees into the Well of Segais (where the Salmon of Knowledge was spawned and spent the early part of its life) were said, according to one account, to pass into the river Boyne either once a year or once in seven years[88] ... and 'those mortals who were fortunate enough to find the nuts and to 'drink the *imbas* out of them' obtained the seer's gift and became accomplished *filid*.'[89]

Irish linguistic scholar Thomas F. O'Rahilly has another notion as to what *teinm laeda* might mean. He suggests that *laeda* is the genitive form not of *laid*, 'poem' but rather *laed*, meaning 'pith' (the flesh or tissue beneath the skin) or 'marrow',[90] a reference to the way in which the boy Finn might have chewed his thumb for divinatory purposes. (See more about Finn's 'tooth of wisdom' *infra*.)

Of Finn's three newly acquired skills, perhaps the best-known is *imbas forosna*, which Meyer translates as 'knowledge which illumines'.[91] O'Donovan's translation of *Sanas Chormaic* gives *Imbas Forosnai* as 'knowledge that enlightens, i.e. it discovers everything which the poet likes and which he desires to manifest'.[92] But much more detail is provided:

> 'Thus it is done. The poet chews a piece of (the) flesh
> of a red pig, or of a dog or cat, and puts it afterwards
> on the flag behind the door, and pronounces an
> incantation on it, and offers it to idol-gods, and

afterwards calls his idols to him and then finds them
not on the morrow, and pronounces incantations on
his two palms, and calls again unto him his idol-gods
that his sleep may not be disturbed; and he lays his
two palms on his two cheeks and (in this manner)
he falls asleep; and he is watched in order that no
one may interrupt [?] nor disturb him till everything
about which he is engaged is revealed to him, (which
may be) a minute or two or three, or as long as he was
supposed to be at (the) offering; et ideo *imbas* dicitur
i.e. (his) two palms (*boiss*) upon (*im*) him, that is (one)
palm over [?] and another hither on his cheeks. Patrick
abolished [banished?] this and the *teinm laegda,* and
he adjudged [testified?] that whoever should practise
them should have neither heaven nor earth, because it
was renouncing baptism.'[93]

Presumably in the case of Finn, he chewed on a
piece of salmon in place of the red pig or dog or cat. A
similar ritual involving the eating of horse or bull flesh is
also well attested.[94] For instance, at Tara a new king was
sometimes chosen in a *tarbfheis,* a 'bull-feast' or 'bull-
sleep', 'in which a bull was killed and a man ate his fill of
its flesh, drank its broth, and then lay down to sleep'.[95]

However, the boy may also have been chewing the
flesh of his own thumb, according to O'Rahilly:

'...whenever Finn wished to renew his wisdom he
had to chew his thumb. An essential part of the
divinatory rite to which Cormac gives the name of
imbas forosnai was the chewing of a piece of the raw
flesh of an animal sacrificed to 'the pagan gods'. In

the same way Finn availed himself of supernatural knowledge whenever he chewed a certain piece of raw flesh, namely, his thumb, which was able to impart divinatory power as a result of its previous contact with the Salmon of Wisdom'.[96]

He may also have been pressing his thumb against a mysterious 'tooth of wisdom' (*dét fís*) in order to access the arcane insights and knowledge.[97] Graves says that in Greek myth, Hermes is given a similar 'divinatory tooth'.[98] In the Irish tale *Fin MacCool, Ceadach Og, and the Fish-Hag,* related by Jeremiah Curtin, in order to find out whether the champion Ceadach Og could be brought back to life, Fin is encouraged to chew his thumb by Diarmuid.

> 'Fin chewed his thumb from the skin to the flesh, from the flesh to the bone, from the bone to the marrow, from the marrow to the juice, and then he knew that there was a sow with three pigs in the Eastern World, and if blood from one of these pigs were put on Ceadach's wound, he would rise up well and healthy.'[99]

The third of the arcane abilities proffered upon the youth Finn after his consumption of the Salmon of Féc is *dichetul dichennaib*, which Meyer translates as 'extempore incantation',[100] i.e. spontaneous, unrehearsed or impromptu singing or exclamations. Cormac's Glossary tells us this was the only one of the three practises that was not banned by Saint Patrick:

> *Dicetal do-chennaib* ('ex-tempore recital'), then, was
> left, to be composed in right of (their) art; for this is
> the cause: it is not necessary in it to make an offering
> to demons, but there is a revelation at once from (the)
> ends of (the poet's) fingers.[101]

Dichetul dichennaib is from the Irish *díchetal,*
'incantation or spell composed extemporaneously by the
filis and druids in ancient Ireland',[102] and *do-cain,* 'chants,
recites (esp. a spell, incantation or magic formula).[103]

One characteristic of Finn's new triad of skills that
appears to link them all is their extemporaneous nature. It
seems that the greatest gift of the new poet is the gift of
spontaneity. He is not to forcefully 'will' these things into
being (although the inspiration can clearly be encouraged
through sucking/chewing his thumb or eating the fish),
but rather to allow something of an unplanned, impulsive
or perhaps intuitive outpouring.

In the second poem about Brug na Bóinde in the
Metrical Dindshenchas, composed by Macnia mac
Oengusa, there is an obscure feature referred to as *Suide
Find,* 'Finn's Seat'.[104] The location of this seat, whatever
it might have been, is not precisely disclosed. It is
mentioned in a passage of several verses referring to the
'vast Matha',[105] a huge monster which was said to have
been killed on a mysterious stone at or near Newgrange
called Lecc Benn.[106] (More on this in 'Killing the
monster', *infra.*)

The salmon and the deity

One of the most extraordinary things written about the Dagda, the chief deity of the Tuatha Dé Danann and first owner of Síd in Broga (Newgrange), is contained in Cináed úa Hartacáin's poem on Brugh na Bóinne preserved in the Book of Leinster.

Úa Hartacáin refers to the Dagda as 'the king of Fíacc's Pool'.[107]

This is an extraordinary and curious claim, one which might seem fatuous or even superfluous given that Dagda is the king of the Tuatha Dé Danann and is described in the poem as the king of Ireland.[108] When you are the owner of Newgrange, possibly the greatest of all Irish monuments, and when you are king of your people, why should one small pool matter a jot when you are the sovereign of all Ireland? The question begged an answer.

For that answer, we must turn again to Cormac's Glossary, and to the work of Thomas F. O'Rahilly. *Sanas Chormaic* tells us that one of the names or epithets of Dagda Mór, king of the Tuatha Dé Danann and king of Fiacc's Pool, was *Ruad-Rofhessa,* meaning 'Lord of great knowledge'.[109] Cormac further tells us that there are two descendants in Dagda's lineage who possess the name *Rofhis* ('Great Knowledge').[110] 'Dagdae Mór,' Whitley Stokes' notes in *Sanas Chormaic* tell us, 'was called the *Ruad rofhessa,* son of all the sciences (*dána*) i.e. a son with whom is all science.'[111]

Earlier, we saw that the alternative name for Fiacc's Pool, Linn Rois, could be derived from *ro-fis*, meaning 'high knowledge' or 'great knowledge'. Dagda's epithet has the same derivation or meaning.

O'Rahilly tells us that some characteristics of an 'Otherworld deity' such as Dagda were his omniscience (*rofhessa,* 'great knowledge') and his polymorphism.[112] The otherworld deity was regularly considered to possess the ability to assume an animal shape, for example a bull, a wolf, a pig, a hawk, an eagle or a swan. However, when the Otherworld was located beneath the sea or a lake or body of water, the deity would take the 'appropriate' shape for a 'denizen of the waters' – a salmon.[113] The mythic exemplar possessing these traits is Fintan Mac Bóchra, who is said to have lived in Ireland before the great flood and who survived for 5,500 years afterwards.[114] Fintan took the form of a salmon at Tul Tuinde (a hill in Tipperary) to avoid the fate of his companions,[115] surviving the flood in that form before assuming the shapes of an eagle and a hawk.[116] One of the rivers where Fintan is said to have lived was the Boyne, where, he remarked, 'short, methought, was my stay'.[117] Fintan was also one-eyed.[118]

MacKillop tells us that the salmon caught by Finn at Linn Féic was named Fintan, but he does not tell us the source.[119] The composer of the Metrical Dindshenchas poem about Temair (Tara) identifies himself as 'Fintan the poet', who declares: 'I am a salmon not of one stream'.[120] Fintan's name is said by some scholars to mean the 'white ancient',[121] or 'white fire',[122] the fire possibly denoting the poetic, creative 'fire in the head' of which Amergin Glúngeal, poet of the Milesians, spoke.[123] The first part of Fintan's name is shared by Finnéces and by the boy Finn too, the whiteness (*finn/find*[124]) having 'certain associations with vision and knowledge as the Common Celtic nominal base **vindo-* 'white',' which derives from an Indo-European root word meaning 'to see (clearly), to know'.[125] Thus, another scholar[126] suggests that Fintan may be 'one of the numerous personifications and late transformations of an archaic deity Find who possesses and imposes hidden knowledge'.[127]

O'Rahilly makes a stronger connection between Dagda and the salmon. The omniscient deity in fish form was known as the *eó fis*, the 'Salmon of Wisdom'.[128] The salmon of Ess Ruaid (Ruad's Waterfall, i.e. the falls of Assaroe on the Erne at Ballyshannon, Co. Donegal), was known as Goll Essa Ruaid,[129] 'The Blind One of Assaroe'.[130] Because it was one-eyed, the salmon, 'as might be expected … is identified with the all-knowing Fintan'.[131] In a masterful piece of scholarship, O'Rahilly tells us the following in relation to Dagda:

> 'Elsewhere we read of a mythical Aed Ruad,[132] who was drowned in the waterfall at Ballyshannon, which from him was called Ess Ruaid, and who left his name also on the adjacent *síd*, or Otherworld-hill, known as Síd Aeda. Here we have the god Aed who presided over the *síd* identified with the Ruad who was drowned in (i.e. who, in pagan belief, lived beneath) the neighbouring waterfall. Another text gives '*Aed Álainn* of Ess Ruaid' as one of the names of the Dagda, who was also known as *In Ruad Rofhessa* and as *Eochaid Ollathair*.'[133]

Aed was another name for the one-eyed Goll mac Morna,[134] who was a long-time adversary of Fionn Mac Cumhaill, having led the killers of Fionn's father, Cumall, at the battle of Cnucha, in which battle he lost his eye.[135]

Fascinatingly, Goll mac Morna is also sometimes later portrayed as a colleague of Fionn.[136] O'Rahilly makes the startling connection between Dagda and the salmon:

> 'From the foregoing evidence it will be sufficiently obvious, without entering into more detailed or more fundamental arguments, that the all-knowing Salmon of Assaroe, *Goll Essa Ruaid*, is identical at once with the all-knowing Dagda and with Goll mac Morna.'[137]

Accepting that this is the case, the claim in úa Hartacáin's poem on Brugh na Bóinne that Dagda was the 'king of Linn Féic' takes on a more meaningful complexion. Dagda is the king of Linn Féic because he is the salmon of Linn Féic.

There are other notable deities and characters who come to fish at Linn Féic. In one tale, the famous warrior Cúchulainn spears a salmon in the river Boyne before mutilating Elcmaire, who had entered the river (specifically at an áth, a ford or shallow point) in order to oppose him.[138] Elsewhere, O'Rahilly points out, there is an account of Cúchulainn 'killing the salmon in Linn Féic'.[139]

'Originally,' says O'Rahilly, 'the spearing of the salmon and the wounding of Elcmaire were one and the same act.'[140] It is notable that both Elcmar/Elcmaire and Dagda were said to be the original owners or custodians of Síd in Broga/Newgrange,[141] and that Elcmar went to the mound at Cleitech overlooking Linn Féic after being dispossessed of Newgrange.[142]

It is noteworthy too that the late Irish folklore scholar Dáithí Ó hÓgáin considered Elcmar and Nuadu to be one and the same deity,[143] and that, in the short tale *Teasmolad Corbmaic úi Cuinn ocus Finn meic Cumhaill sunn*, 'Here is the Panegyric of Conn's son Cormac and the Death of Finn son of Cumhaill', Finn was declared to be a 'great-grandson to Nuada Necht'.[144]

Ó hÓgáin says that while the origin of the name of Nechtain (owner of Nechtain's Well (Segais), the source of the Boyne, and husband of Bóinn[145]) is unclear, it is probably related to an ancient word for water, *necht*.[146] Nuadu, Nechtain and Elcmar were, Ó hÓgáin argues, the same deity with different names.[147] But he goes further, and makes a fascinating connection with the story of the salmon of Linn Féic by telling us that 'the full name' of the seer Finnéces was Nuadhu Finneigéas, and that the story was 'obviously suggested by the myth of how the youngster called Mac Óg got the dwelling of Newgrange from Nuadhu'.[148]

And thus, in the lore of Brú na Bóinne, we have two stories of youngsters winning a great prize from their seniors – Oengus gains the *Brugh* from Elcmar/Nuadu/Nechtain/Dagda and Finn gains the Salmon of Féc from Finnégas.

In terms of links between Finn and Nuadu, Ó hÓgáin says: 'The whole development can best be explained by supposing that the image of Nuadhu and his fish was super-imposed onto the earlier lore of Fionn's wisdom.'[149] One result of this connection was the frequent designation of Nuadhu as 'Nuadhu Find', and a further development of this fusion, Ó hÓgáin suggests, was making Nuadhu a maternal ancestor to Fionn.[150]

Another of the enigmatic characters of early Irish narrative is Cú Roí (hound of the plain?)[151] who is a hero,

Figure 6: Síd in Broga (Newgrange), which the youth Oengus won from much more elder deities. Photo by the author.

a divinity, a king, a chief, a wizard and a traveller. In the tale *Aided Con Roí* (the Violent Death of Cú Roí), it is related that in order to kill him, Cúchulainn has first to kill a certain salmon in a well, using Cú Roí's own sword, before turning the weapon on its owner. Cú Roí's soul resides in the salmon, and when Cúchulainn kills the fish Cú Roí loses his strength and bravery.[152] Cú Roí was able to take many forms, but in *Aided Con Roí* he has to be killed first in salmon-form and then as a human.[153]

Might the salmon have been a substitute for something else? In the prose Dindshenchas, in the tale about Crotta Cliach, we read about a dragon in a lake in the shape of a salmon.[154] Cliach the harper tries to entice the daughter of Búidhb from Síd Fear Feimin, but after a year of music-making, the ground beneath him bursts open and a dragon emerges. Cliach dies of terror. Ternóc's foster mother later finds the 'dragon of fire … in a salmon's shape' and Fursa drives it into the lake,[155] from where, in dragon form, it is 'prophesied to arise on St. John's day at the end of the world and afflict Ireland in vengeance for John the Baptist'.[156]

O'Rahilly suggests that the story of Finn eating the Salmon of Wisdom is an 'Irish modification of the widespread belief that wisdom could be acquired by eating a sacred serpent'.[157] Because serpents or snakes were not known in Ireland, the substitution of salmon for serpent 'was a natural one',[158] he contends. As an aside, the widespread folk belief that Saint Patrick drove the snakes out of Ireland might be the reverberation of earlier motifs in which a deity slays a fish, snake or serpent.[159] O'Rahilly entices us to compare Finn's slaying of his enemy, the one-eyed sun god Goll, with Lugh's heroic slaying of the one-eyed Balor at the Second Battle of Moytura.[160]

Another scholar, Proinsias MacCana, goes further in connecting Finn and Lugh. He points out that Finn's defeat of a terrifying being named Aillén mac Midhna who burned down the royal court of Tara every Samhain makes him the 'vanquisher of a supernatural one-eyed burner'.[161] Balar/Balor could burn things with his baleful eye, and was known to turn humans and animals to stone just by opening his great eyelid.[162]

One tale from Co. Mayo relates that Balar 'had a single eye in his forehead, a venomous fiery eye. There were always seven coverings over his eye. One by one Balar removed the coverings. With the first covering the bracken began to wither, with the second the grass became copper-coloured, with the third the woods and timber began to heat, with the fourth smoke came from the trees, with the fifth everything grew red, with the sixth it sparked. With the seventh they were all set on fire, and the whole countryside was ablaze!'[163]

'There is here an obvious analogy,' says MacCana, 'with the myth of Lugh's defeat of Balar of the evil eye and this analogy may be more than mere coincidence. For in point of fact there are considerable grounds for believing that Fionn was himself divine.'[164]

'The fact that the same basic theme appears to underlie several of the earliest tales of Fionn as is found in the myth of Lugh's destruction of Balar seems to corroborate these indications. Indeed there are various other analogies between the traditions of Fionn, 'The Fair One', and Lugh, 'The Bright One', and it has been suggested – not implausibly – that Fionn may originally have been another name for the god Lugh.'[165]

The eponymous goddess of the Boyne river, Bóinn, is deprived of an eye when she approaches the Well of Segais (Nechtain's Well),[166] causing the water to gush forth and create the river. This might, suggests author Patricia Monaghan, reflect 'a common connection of inner vision and outer blindness, as well as connecting her through the motif of the single eye with the famous resident of the river source, the one-eyed salmon sometimes called Fintan'.[167]

Killing the monster

In the mythology of Brú na Bóinne, and in particular in the Dindshenchas, we have references to a great monster, which appears to be some type of huge water snake or centipede. It is given a name, spelt variously as Mata, Máta, Matae and Mátha.[168]

This monster is difficult to describe as its appearance is not consistent in the manuscripts. In the Prose Dindshenchas description of *Dindgnai in Broga*, 'The Remarkable Things of the Brug', it is related that the monster was 'a tortoise'[169], while the same story just a couple of sentences later suggests the creature had 'seven score feet … and seven heads'.[170] A strange beast indeed!

The Metrical Dindshenchas poem about Áth Clíath Cúalann also describes it as having seven score feet, but only four heads instead of seven.[171]

Accounts differ too as to how the strange beast was killed. Having 'licked up Boyne till it became a valley'[172] it was then 'slain on Brug maic ind Oc',[173] suggesting that it was killed on or at the Newgrange monument.[174]

The Metrical Dindshenchas poem Brug na Bóinde II relates that it was the 'mighty Ulstermen' who broke the limbs of the Mata.[175] However, in the tale *Tochmarc Emire*, 'The Wooing of Emer', the honour of killing the beast is reserved for the Dagda:

> '…it is from this that it is called the Plain of Murthemne, viz., a magic sea was on it with […] in it, so that one could sit on it, so that a man with his armour might sit down on the ground of […] until

Figure 7: Dagda's Mound and Newgrange. The Mata was killed on or at Newgrange, according to the Dinshenchas.

the Dagda came with his club of anger, and sang the following words at it, so that it ebbed away at once:
Silent thy hollow head,
Silent thy dirty body,
Silent thy [...] brow.'[176]

The beast was a slow-moving creature, and seems to have dwelt in the river itself, or alternatively it occupied the river valley having licked up the river.

Know ye by the refuse of heads
the Glen where the sluggish Matha dwelt?[177]

Given some of the descriptions of it, the Mata sounds like something called an *oillphéist* (from *oll*, great and *péist*, a fabulous beast or reptile), a 'Dragon-like monster from Irish oral tradition'.[178] In fact, in a story almost identical to the Mata licking up the Boyne, the route of river Shannon was said to have been formed by an *oillphéist* 'when Saint Patrick has come to drive out its kind'.[179]

Given that the dragon or 'worm' is 'only a magnified serpent',[180] and that the serpent or snake never existed in Ireland, could we propose that the tale of the Dagda killing the Mata at the Boyne or Saint Patrick driving out the *oillphéist* of the river Shannon are variants of the story of the spearing of the salmon by the hero or deity? There is nothing, admittedly, in the story of the Mata about the Dagda eating the monster! In fact, the beast's body is dismembered and thrown into the Boyne, where large chunks of it float away and form new landscape features such as the Boyne Estuary (Inber Colpa, from *colptha,* its shinbone) and the ford of Dublin.[181] In essence, the story of the Mata is a creation myth, from the branch of such stories in which the new world is created from the pieces of a dismembered monster or deity.[182]

There are other legends of water monsters in Ireland. In a tale reminiscent of the killing of the Mata at the mysterious stone of Lecc Benn at Newgrange, Saint Colmcille was said to have driven a monster into a lake in Donegal and tied it to a stone there.[183] The story relates that Colmcille was surrounded by the beast (in this case spelt *ullphéist*) and that the saint tied the monster to a slab of rock on a hill called Cnoc Chró, before pushing the creature into Loch Doire-Bheatha.[184]

There were no monsters in the river Boyne when Amergin, the bard and spiritual figurehead of the Milesians, arrived at its estuary.[185] However, as he put his right foot on the shore, he chanted a poem, the words of which have often been quoted, but one line of which stands out in the context of our exploration of the story of Finn:

Am he i l-lind
I am Salmon in Pool[186]

Then, 'Amorgen sang also at that time to drive fishes into creeks'.[187] This brought an eruption of fish, a 'white flash'.[188]

Íascach muir!	A fishful sea!
Mothach tír!	A fertile land!
Tomaidm n-éisc!	An eruption of fish!
Íasc fo tuind	Fish under wave
I rethaib én!	Streams of birds!
Fairrge cruaid!	A rough sea!
Cassar find	A white flash
Cétaib iach	Hundreds of salmon
Lethan Míl!	A broad whale!
Portach laid—	A harbour-song—
'Tomaidm n-éisc,	'An eruption of fish,
Íascach muir!'	A fishful sea!'[189]

Clearly there is something about the salmon in the Boyne connected with wisdom and poetry. Amergin, as the poet of the Milesians (and not their military leader) had negotiated directly with the tutelary goddesses of Ireland, and he seems to have won their hearts. His landing, according to the second redaction of the story of the Sons of Mil in Lebor Gabála Érenn, occurred at Inver Colpa, the estuary of the Boyne which was said to have been formed when the shinbone (colptha) of the Mata had floated there.

The boon and peril of the deep pool

The Swiss psychoanalyst C.G. Jung maintained that water in dreams and myth symbolised the dark psyche and the unconscious, which, lying underneath consciousness, is often referred to as the 'subconscious'.[190]

'Water is,' Jung wrote, '… a living symbol of the dark psyche.'[191] In fact, he stated: 'Water is the commonest symbol for the unconscious.'[192] In his landmark work *The Archetypes and the Collective Unconscious*, Jung helps bring psychological meaning to the imagery of Fiacc's Pool and the magic fish that is concealed in its deep, dark waters.

'Man's descent to the water is needed,' Jung writes, 'in order to evoke the miracle of its coming to life.'[193]

Indeed, the waters conceal a treasure of sorts, a 'precious inheritance'.[194] 'We must surely go the way of the waters, which always tend downward, if we would raise up the treasure.'[195]

A Gnostic hymn to the soul, contained in the Apocryphal New Testament, relates how a boy is sent by his parents to seek a pearl that fell from the king's crown. The pearl lies at the bottom of a deep well, where it is guarded by a dragon.[196] In this hymn, we are reminded of the magic *cnó*, the hazel nuts that fall from the trees which are said to grow over the Boyne's source well at Segais,[197] and sometimes over the pool where the salmon resides in the Boyne.[198] These are the sacred nuts upon which the great salmon feeds in order to gain its great knowledge. The *cnó* fall down into the waters of the unconscious, where they are consumed by the creature that is to be the boon of the one who would fish in the waters of his own dark nature.

The nine hazels of Crimall the sage
drop their fruits yonder under the well:
they stand by the power of magic spells
under a darksome mist of wizardry.

When the cluster of nuts is ripe
they fall down into the well:
they scatter below on the bottom,
and the salmon eat them.

From the juice of the nuts (no paltry matter)
they form the mystic bubbles;
thence come momently the bubbles
down the green-flowing streams.[199]

The fish also represents a symbol of the saviour
or the bringer of healing (in Finn's case, wisdom).
'Mankind looked and waited,' writes Jung, 'and it was
a *fish*— 'levatus de profundo' (drawn from the deep) —
that became the symbol of the saviour, the bringer of
healing.'[200] The fish that Finnéces draws from the depths
of Fiacc's Pool is the boon for which the youngster
Finn is destined. He discards his old name, *Deimhne,*
'certainty', in favour of the bright whiteness of his new
name, *Finn,* representing the lustrous, shining nature
of one who has seen into the darkest pools of his own
psyche.

The descent into the depths, i.e. the pools and deep
waters of the unconscious, represented in the legend
of Finn by the act of seeking the treasured fish, always
precedes an ascent. According to Jung:

'Here again the dreamer, thirsting for the shining heights, had first to descend into the dark depths, and this proves to be the indispensable condition for climbing any higher.'[201]

There is a trial of heroism, a test of courage involved in coming to the deep water and reaching down into its murky depths.

'...whoever looks into the mirror of the water will see first of all his own face. Whoever goes to himself risks a confrontation with himself. The mirror does not flatter, it faithfully shows whatever looks into it; namely, the face we never show to the world because we cover it with the persona, the mask of the actor.'[202]

It was precisely this confrontation that the eponymous river goddess Bóinn experienced when she approached Nechtain's Well (Segais), the place where the salmon had been born and grew up on the bubbles of wisdom. She approached the well, which was guarded by the king and his three cup-bearers, (i.e. an all-male domain) and made a 'trial of its power'[203] by looking into it. She walked three times around it, and three giant waves burst from it, depriving her of a foot, an eye and a hand, before carrying her out to sea (while forming the river Boyne), where she was drowned.[204]

The confrontation with one's own shadow is 'sufficient to frighten off most people', Jung says, and such confrontation can be avoided when we project the more unpleasant and negative aspects of ourselves into the environment.[205] However, meeting with one's own shadow can also result in disaster, because 'nothing is more disillusioning than the discovery of our own inadequacy'.[206]

> 'The shadow is a tight passage, a narrow door, whose painful constriction no one is spared who goes down to the deep well. But one must learn to know oneself in order to know who one is. For what comes after the door is, surprisingly enough, a boundless expanse full of unprecedented uncertainty … It is the world of water, where all life floats in suspension…'[207]

For Finn, the dark pool has an unprecedented boon – the *imbas* or *fis* which brings to him all knowledge, i.e. not the prognosticative and telepathic powers that ordinary mortals sometimes long to possess, but rather the full knowledge of one's own human depths, of one's genius and one's ineptitude, one's skills and one's weaknesses, the knowledge of which brings true wisdom to one's experiences in the wide world and among other fallible humans.

'A secret life holds sway in the unconscious,' writes Jung.[208] Perhaps all those who have dreamed of the Salmon of Knowledge '…know that the treasure lies in the depths of the water and will try to salvage it'.[209] But they must do it in a way that does not imperil their consciousness, and must anchor themselves to the earth so as to 'become fishers who catch with hook and net what swims in the water'.[210]

The well of Segais, in which the salmon is spawned and grows on the magic nuts of wisdom is, perhaps, in the words of Joseph Campbell, 'the World Navel, its flaming water the indestructible essence of existence'.[211]

Figure 8: The view over Fiacc's Pool from the grounds of Rossnaree House (Cleitech) towards Newgrange.

The boon of Linn Féic is realised by Finn, who consumes the magic salmon and, being initiated into a world of new knowledge, foresight and wisdom, assumes the mantle of his master, tutor and guide Finnéces – 'Finn the Seer'.

There is something in the story of the death of the illustrious High King, Cormac mac Airt, at Cleitech that reminds us that the salmon fished from the depths of the pool of the unconscious does not always provide nourishment for the growth of the human soul. For it is recorded in the Annals of the Four Masters that, in the year 266AD, Cormac 'died at Cleiteach, the bone of a salmon sticking in his throat'.[212]

After Cormac had converted to Christianity, he 'turned against the Druids', and on account of his deference to the Christian God in preference to them, the druid Maelgenn incited the *siabhradh* (spectres, phantoms or supernatural beings[213]) against him, and a devil attacked him and 'gave him a painful death'.[214]

Describing Cormac as 'absolutely the best king that ever reigned in Ireland before himself', the Annals of Clonmacnoise record that the 'Priest of the Golden Calfe (druid) … made a Salmon bone stick fast in his throat until it choked him' and he died in one of his manor houses 'called the house of Cleiteagh near the River of Boyne'.[215]

> There came not Cormac free from sorrow:
> after receiving the Truth (he affirmed it)
> he found repose above limpid Boyne
> on the shore at Rossnaree.[216]

Given that both Cormac and Finn died in proximity to the Boyne, and to Fiacc's Pool, it is perhaps fitting to note that Finn was keeper of Cormac's dogs:

> 'Now he whom Cormac had for chief of the household and for stipendiary master of the hounds was Finn son of Cumhall; for the primest leader that the king of Ireland had was his master of the hounds always.'[217]

The death of Finn

Finn was, according to one tradition, 'slain with a fishing-gaff'.[218] According to the Annals of the Four Masters, in the year 283AD, 'Finn was killed, it was with darts, With a lamentable wound.'[219] O'Donovan notes that: 'It is stated in the Dublin copy of the Annals of Innisfallen that Finn Mac Cumhail, the celebrated general of the Irish militia, fell by the hands of Athlach, son of Duibhdrenn, a treacherous fisherman, who [fired with the love of everlasting notoriety] slew him with his gaff at Rath-Breagha, near the Boyne, whither he had retired in his old age to pass the remainder of his life in tranquillity.'[220] Athlach's notoriety was shortlived, however, because he was 'soon after beheaded by Caeilte Mac Ronain, the relative and faithful follower of Finn'.[221]

Finn's death is also mentioned in the Dindshenchas of Brug na Bóinde:

> At the Trench of the gentle Seagulls
> it is there was wrought the deed—
> great the proud feat of the spear—
> the slaying of Finn whom the bold Luagne smote.[222]

The 'Luagne' mentioned here refers to the Lúagni Temrach, a tribe against whom Finn was battling at the time of his death. The name of Athlach, his killer, is also rendered Aiclech mac Dubdrenn,[223] who cut off his head, according to the Annals of Tigernach:

46

Figure 9: An Atlantic salmon jumping the floodgate at Slane, a few kilometres upstream from Linn Féic.

> Find, grandson of Baiscne, was beheaded by Aichlech, son of Dubdriu, and by the sons of Uirgriu, of the Luaigni of Tara, at Áth Brea on the Boyne.[224]

Finn foresaw his own demise, according to the tale of the Death of Finn.[225] By the greatest irony, he saw his own end by putting his thumb under his *dét fis:*

> 'Under his 'knowledge-tooth' (*fó déd fis*) he put his thumb then, and worked the incantation of *teinm laeghda,* whereby it was revealed to him that the end of his term and of his life was come...'[226]

He had come, says another tale, in his old age to make one final test of his failing strength by attempting to jump across the river Boyne, at a spot which bore the name 'Léim Finn', or 'Finn's Leap'.[227]

47

'It is old age the men notice on me. I (shall) know that by my running and leaping, for it is in the east my 'Leap' is, even on the Boyne, and I shall go to its brink.'[228]

Perhaps he was trying to imitate the salmon, which, when they come in from the sea, jump out of the water in an attempt to dislodge the sea-lice which often infect them. In his own poem, sung after he eats the Salmon of Knowledge (see appendix 1), Finn says: '…the speckled fish leaps, strong is the bound of the swift warrior'.

There is an alternative tale as to how Finn met his demise. The tale is found in a manuscript fragment (Egerton 92, folio 6a) and reads: 'Then he went along the Boyne eastward until he reached his 'Leap'. Thereupon he fell between two rocks, so that his forehead struck against the rock and his brains were dashed about him, and he died between the two rocks.'[229]

Perhaps unsurprisingly, his body was found by 'Fishermen of the Boyne' (*iascaire na Boinde*).[230]

And thus it is that we can say that Finn was born (to the extent that he was initiated into a new life by consuming the salmon, shedding his old name Demne) and died by the banks of his beloved river Boyne.

END

Miscellanea

In *Altram Tige Dá Medar,* after Eithne is separated from her Dé Danann kinsfolk, she meets a cleric who goes to the river with his angling rod and catches her a 'very beautiful salmon, and he had never seen the like of it … and it was an effort for him to carry it from the river to the church'.[231] One wonders if this cleric was perhaps an ascetic, living a lonely life by the Boyne, like the seer Finnéces, who Macgnímartha Find says had been seven years by the Boyne, 'watching the salmon of Fec's Pool' before the boy Demne had come to him.[232]

The 'joyous cleric' of *Altram Tige Dá Medar,* like Finnéces, is a threshold guardian of sorts who will guide the neophyte Eithne (who was previously one of the Tuatha Dé Danann) into the 'new knowledge' (wisdom) of Christianity.

She asks the cleric what his occupation is. He replies: 'Praising the Lord and reading aloud in this book', and she asks him to become her teacher, and to 'give me a lesson every day'.[233] The cleric encourages her to resolutely memorise what is in the little psalter, and thus Eithne, like Finn, is, one could say, learning poetry from the priest/druid. She learns from the book diligently, 'as if she had been learning it from the night she was born'.[234] It is then that they eat salmon together. First the cleric catches a salmon, but there is not enough for both of them, so he returns to the river and drops his hook and a short time later catches an extraordinary salmon.[235] This is the fish that Eithne eats.

There is a sad end to the tale, however. After receiving the faith, Eithne sees Oengus and her kinfolk on the other side of the river, seeking for her, but they can no longer see her. She is heartbroken, and her health declines. She asks that Saint Patrick baptize her and pardon her sins, which is granted and she dies in his bosom.

---<><><>---

Oisín was Finn Mac Cumhaill's most famous son. Oisín's mother Blaí (one of the wives of Finn) lived at Cleitech. In *Acallam na Senórach,* we are told that 'Oisín went to the *Síd* of the Breast of Cleitech, where his mother, Blaí, daughter of Derg Díanscothach 'the Quick of Speech', lived.[236] In other words, Finn's wife and the mother of his illustrious son Oisín lived in close proximity to Fiacc's Pool.

One can only assume that the *síd* on the breast of Cleitech was the same mound to which Elcmar retired after being dispossessed of Síd in Broga by Oengus. Cleitech has its own poem in the Metrical Dindshenchas, which relates that its 'revered name' derives from a druid called Cleitech who was buried there.[237] Cleitech is referred to in the MD poem as '*cléithe tech nÉrend uile*', which is translated as 'the top of all houses' in Erin.[238]

Appendix

1: Finn's lay

Here is the lay that Finn made after he had consumed the Salmon of Knowledge, to 'prove his poetry':

> May-day, season surpassing! Splendid is colour then.
> Blackbirds sing a full lay, if there be a slender shaft of day.
> The dust-coloured cuckoo calls aloud: Welcome, splendid summer! The bitterness of bad weather is past, the boughs of the wood are a thicket.
> Summer cuts the river down, the swift herd of horses seeks the pool, the long hair of the heather is outspread, the soft white bog-down grows.
> Panic startles the heart of the deer, the smooth sea runs apace,—season when ocean sinks asleep,— blossom covers the world.
> Bees with puny strength carry a goodly burden, the harvest of blossoms; up the mountain-side kine take with them mud, the ant makes a rich meal.
> The harp of the forest sounds music, the sail gathers— perfect peace. Colour has settled on every height, haze on the lake of full waters.
> The corncrake, a strenuous bard, discourses; the lofty virgin waterfall sings a welcome to the warm pool; the talk of the rushes is come.
> Light swallows dart aloft, loud melody reaches round the hill, the soft rich mast buds, the stuttering quagmire rehearses.

The peat-bog is as the raven's coat, the loud cuckoo bids welcome, the speckled fish leaps, strong is the bound of the swift warrior.

Man flourishes, the maiden buds in her fair strong pride; perfect each forest from top to ground, perfect each great stately plain.

Delightful is the season's splendour, rough winter has gone, white is every fruitful wood, a joyous peace is summer.

A flock of birds settles in the midst of meadows; the green field rustles, wherein is a brawling white stream. A wild longing is on you to race horses, the ranked host is ranged around: a bright shaft has been shot into the land, so that the water-flag is gold beneath it. A timorous tiny persistent little fellow sings at the top of his voice, the lark sings clear tidings: surpassing May-day of delicate colours![239]

2 Oral versions of the Salmon of Knowledge story

The following oral versions of the story of the Salmon of Knowledge are reproduced here from the Schools' Collection of the National Folklore Collection at University College Dublin (UCD).

Long ago there lived in Ireland a man named Fionn Mc Cuil. When he was a young boy he was taught by a man name Finegas. At that time there was a strange salmon in the Boyne and Finegas wanted for years to catch it. He happened to catch him one day. He gave it to Fionn to roast. Fionn did so and when turning it he touched the fish with his finger and burned it. He then put his finger in his mouth to cure it. The virtue of the Salmon

of Knowledge entered Fionn and all he had to do was to put his finger in his mouth when he wanted to know anything.
– Told by Maud Kelly, Edenbaun, Co. Sligo.[240]

There was once a wise man named Fingas who lived on the banks of the Boyne. This man wanted to catch a fish "called the Salmon of Knowledge". Fingas caught the salmon. He felt the salmon on the pan & left a youth named Fionn to mind it. He told the boy not to touch it. After a while a blister rose on the salmon and the boy put his thumb on it to put it down. In doing this he burned his thumb any day Fionn wants to know any Knowledge he put his thumb in his mouth.
– Told by Peggy Byrne, Fair Street, Drogheda, to Patty Newman.[241]

One fine afternoon as Fionn and a bard sat on the banks of the river Boyne a salmon came leaping into the river. "Catch the salmon" said the bard and when you have done so roast and bring it to me but eat none of it. Fionn did as he was bidden and when he brought the fish to the bard, the bard asked him did he eat any of the fish. Fionn said no but that had burned his thumb in turning the salmon. He said that he put his thumb into his mouth. Then said the bard you have tasted the salmon of knowledge. After this Fionn whenever he wished to discover anything he put his burned thumb to his lips and then nothing remained hidden from him.[242]

---<><><>---

Long ago there lived a man in Slane called Feg. He lived beside a deep part of the Boyne, down beside the Bridge. There was a well some where around Slane and it is not known where it was. The river that Feg lived beside was fed by that well. There was a Salmon living in the well called the Salmon of Knowledge. There was a tree of hazel nuts growing over the well, and the people were forbidden to eat them. When the nuts would fall into the well the Salmon would eat them. There was a woman called Boann and she said she would get them: and she did. Some kind of an earthquake came and the Salmon got out of the well, and went down the little stream that was leading down to Feg's pool and went into Feg's pool and there Fionn caught it.[243]

---<><><>---

In olden times there were many saints in Ireland. St. Erc was our local saint he lived on the bank of the Boyne in an old hut which he made himself after giving up the teaching.

The saint died after a while and was supposed to be buried in this hut. After many years a man named Fionn came to live on the banks of the Boyne. He came here to catch the Salmon of Knowledge. There is a story told about it. One day as he was fishing a little boy came running along the bank. His name was also Fionn. The old Fionn caught the salmon, he left the boy to cook the Salmon. When the fish was nearly cooked the boy put his finger into the pot it was so hot that it burned him he put his finger in his mouth and he became wise. When the old Fionn heard this he was vexed and sent the boy away. – *Told by Patrick Brien, Slane, Co. Meath.*[244]

---<><><>---

At one time there lived a famous body of heroes in Ireland known as the Fianna Eireann or the Fenians of Erin, Fionn Mac Cuail was their chief.

Fionn's boyhood was spent int the wild woods of the Slieve Bloom mountains. There he was trained to hunt and fish and throw the spear and also he was fond of learning, of poetry and of music. In these subjects an old bard, named Finnegan became his teacher.

One time afternoon, as they sat by the river, master and pupil together, a salmon came leaping into a pool at their feet.

"Catch the fish," said Finnegan, "and when you have caught it, roast it by the fire. When it is cooked, eat none of it, but bring it straight to me."

Fionn promised to obey. He caught the salmon and roasted it and carried it to his teacher, who had gone to his hut. The old man asked Fionn did he eat any of it. "No," answered Fionn. I never told a lie. But when I was turning the salmon before the fire, the hot skin burned my thumb, and a little of the skin may have stuck to it. I just put my thumb in my mouth to ease the pain.

"Then," said Finnegan, "you have tasted of the Salmon of Knowledge by accident, you have been the first to taste it. Take the fish and eat it Fionn, son of Cual, for to you the gift shall be given, and not to me. Now go away from this place, there is nothing more I can teach you." Fionn became possessed of all knowledge. Whenever he wanted to know anything he put the thumb that was burned into his lips and nothing remained hidden from him.[245]

---<><><>---

The following version of the tale was related to Anna Lee, Cratloe Cross, Co. Clare:

Long ago there was a party of brave, fearless men known as the Fenians or the Fianna. There are many stories told about these.

This is one relating to Fionn, about how he got his name "Fionn". Diana as was his name first had a teacher named Fingas and he caught the Salmon of Knowledge in the River Boyne. One day when he was roasting the salmon Diana came in and Fingas told him to mind the salmon but not to eat any of it. Diana was turning the salmon and he burned his thumb. He then stuck his thumb in his mouth to ease the pain. At that moment all knowledge came to Diana. Fingas then said he could teach him no more, and told him his name should be Fionn. When he wanted to know anything all he had to do was to put his thumb in his mouth and chew it.[246]

Acknowledgements

The front cover photo shows an Atlantic salmon jumping over one of the weirs on the river Boyne. I am indebted to Aubrey Martin of Perfect Stills Photography for graciously allowing me to use this fabulous photo.

I am grateful to University College Dublin for permission to reproduce the folk versions of the story of the Salmon of Knowledge from the National Folklore Collection.

I acknowledge the diligent work of generations of scholars and philologists who pored over our ancient manuscripts and translated them, an arduous and time-consuming task. It is only because of their work that publications such as this are possible.

I extend my gratitude to author Morgan Daimler who kindly translated a passage from Irish for this monograph. (See footnote 128). Thanks to Mandy McKerl for proofreading the text and suggesting changes and improvements.

This work, and indeed much of the work of Mythical Ireland, is helped enormously by the generous support of the Mythical Ireland patrons at www.patreon.com/mythicalireland. Please consider becoming a patron to help bring more of this published work to frution.

– Anthony Murphy, Drogheda, April 2021

Bibliography

AC: Annals of Clonmacnoise. Murphy, Rev. Denis, S.J. (1896), *The Annals of Clonmacnoise being Annals of Ireland from the Earliest Period to A.D. 1408,* University Press, Dublin.

AFM: Annals of the Four Masters. *Annals of the Kingdom of Ireland, by the Four Masters, from the earliest period to the year 1616,* edited and translated by John O'Donovan, in two volumes, Hodges, Smith and Co., Dublin.

Anecdota: Bergin, O.J., Best, R.I., Meyer, Kuno & O'Keeffe, J.G. *Anecdota from Irish Manuscripts,* Vols. I-V, Hodges, Figgis & Co. Ltd., Dublin, 1907-1913.

Best, R.I. and Bergin, Osborn (eds) (1929), *Lebor na hUidre: Book of the Dun Cow,* Royal Irish Academy. (Reprinted 1970).

Bondarenko, Grigory (2012), *Fintan mac Bóchra: Irish synthetic history revisited*, in: Fomin, Maxim, Václav Blažek, and Piotr Stalmaszczyk (eds), Transforming traditions: studies in archaeology, comparative linguistics and narrative: proceedings of the Fifth International Colloquium of Societas Celto-Slavica, held at Příbram, 26–29 July 2010, Studia Celto-Slavica 6, Łódź: Łódź University Press, 2012

Borlase, William (1897), *The Dolmens of Ireland, Volume II,* Chapman & Hall Ltd., London.

Campbell, Joseph (1988) [1949], *The Hero With a Thousand Faces,* Paladin Books.

Curtin, Jeremiah (1894), *Hero-Tales of Ireland,* MacMillan and Co., London.

Dooley, Ann and Roe, Harry (trans.) (2008)[1999], *Tales of the Elders of Ireland,* Oxford World's Classics.

Duncan, Lilian (1932), *Altram Tige Dá Medar,* Ériu, Vol. 11., pp. 184-225.

Freund, Philip (2003), *Myths of Creation,* Peter Owen Publishers.

Gantz, Jeffrey (1981), *Early Irish Myths and Sagas,* Penguin Books.

Graves, Robert (1990) [1955], *The Greek Myths,* in two volumes, Penguin Books.

Graves, Robert (1999) [1948], *The White Goddess: A Historical Grammar of Poetic Myth,* faber and faber.

Gwynn, Lucius (1914), *Cináed úa Hartacáin's Poem on Brugh na* Bóinne, Ériu, Vol. 7.

Hennessy, William M., (1887), *Annals of Ulster. Otherwise Annala Senait, Annals of Senat; A Chronicle of Irish Affairs from A.D. 431 to A.D. 1540,* Vol. I.

Hensey, Robert (2015), *First Light: The Origins of Newgrange,* Oxbow Books.

Hickey, Elizabeth (2000) [1966], *I Send My Love Along the Boyne,* republished by Áine Ni Chairbre, Drogheda.

Hogan, Edmund, S.J. (1910), *Onomasticon Goedelicum: An Index, with Identifications, to the Gaelic Names of Places and Tribes,* Hodges, Figgis & Co., Limited, Dublin.

Holten, Anthony (2016), *The River Boyne: Hidden legacies, history and lore explored on foot and by boat,* self-published.

Jung, C.G. (1990)[1959], *The Archetypes and the Collective Unconscious,* Princeton University Press.

Kalygin, V.P., (2002), *'Kel'tskaya kosmologiya' ['Celtic Cosmology'],* in: Mikhaylova, T.A.. Kalygin V. P. & Toporova T.V., eds., Predstavleniya o smerti i lokalizatsiya inogo mira u kel'tov i germantsev [Images of Death and Localisation of the Otherworld in Celtic and Germanic Traditions], Moscow: Yazyki slavyanskoy kul'tury, 82-109.

LGE: Lebor Gabála Érenn. Macalister, R.A.S. (1938-1956), *Lebor Gabála Érenn, The Book of the Taking of Ireland,* five volumes, Irish Texts Society.

MacCana, Proinsias (1973)[1970], *Celtic Mythology,* Hamlyn.

MacKillop, James (1998), *Oxford Dictionary of Celtic Mythology,* Oxford University Press.

MD: *Metrical Dindshenchas,* published in five parts (1903-1935), translated by Edward Gwynn and published originally by the Royal Irish Academy, now available from the School of Celtic Studies, Dublin Institute for Advanced Studies.

Meyer, Kuno (1888), *The Wooing of Emer,* in The Archaeological Review, Vol. I, David Nutt, London.

Meyer, Kuno (1904), *The Boyish Exploits of Finn*, in Ériu: The Journal of the School of Irish Learning, Dublin, Vol. I.

Monaghan, Patricia (2004), *The Encyclopedia of Celtic Mythology and Folklore,* Facts On File., Inc.

Murphy, Anthony (2018), *The Dagda and Cosmology in the Early Stories of Brug na Bóinne,* in Harp, Club & Cauldron: A Harvest of Knowledge – a curated anthology of scholarship, lore, and creativity on the Dagda in Irish tradition, edited by Lora O'Brien and Morpheus Ravenna, Eel & Otter Press.

Murphy, Anthony (2019), *Dronehenge: The Story Behind the Remarkable Discovery at Newgrange,* Liffey Press.

Murphy, Anthony and Moore, Richard (2020)[2006], *Island of the Setting Sun: In Search of Ireland's Ancient Astronomers,* Liffey Press, Dublin.

Murphy, Anthony (2021), *Return to Segais,* self-published.

O'Donovan, John (trans.) and Stokes, Whitley (Ed.) (1868), *Sanas Chormaic, Cormac's Glossary, edited, with notes and indices by Whitley Stokes*, Printed by O.T Cutter, Calcutta, for the Irish Archaeological and Celtic Society.

O'Grady, Standish (1892), *Silva Gadelica: A Collection of Tales in Irish,* in two volumes, Williams and Norgate, London.

Ó hÓgáin, Dáithí (1991), *Myth, Legend & Romance: An Encyclopaedia of the Irish Folk Tradition,* Prentice Hall Press.

O'Meara, John F. (trans.) (1982)[1951], *Gerald of Wales: The History and Topography of Ireland,* Penguin Classics.

O'Rahilly, Cecile (2006) [1976], *Táin Bó Cúailnge, Recension 1,* Dublin Institute for Advanced Studies.

O'Rahilly, Thomas F. (1946), *Early Irish History and Mythology,* School of Celtic Studies, Dublin Institute for Advanced Studies (2010 reprint).

OSL Meath: *Ordnance Survey Letters Meath, edited with an introduction by Michael Herity MRIA,* Four Masters Press, Dublin, 2001.

RC: *Revue Celtique,* a French academic journal on Celtic studies based in Paris, published in 52 volumes between 1870 and 1934.

Rees, Alwyn & Rees, Brinley (1961), *Celtic Heritage: Ancient tradition in Ireland and Wales,* Thames and Hudson.

Rolleston, T.W. (1910), *The High Deeds of Finn and Other Bardic Romances of Ancient Ireland,* Harrap, London.

Stokes, Whitley (1894-95), *The Prose Tales in the Rennes Dindshenchas,* published in *Revue Celtique* vols. XV (1894) and XVI (1895), pp. 272-336, 418-484; 31-83, 135-167, 269-312.

Stout, Geraldine (2002), *Newgrange and the Bend of the Boyne,* Cork University Press.

Went, Arthur E.J., (1953) *Material for a history of the fisheries of the River Boyne,* County Louth Archaeological Journal XIII.

ZCP: *Zeitschrift für Celtische Philologie,* (Journal of Celtic Philology) founded by Kuno Meyer and Ludwig Christian Stern, published annually from 1897.

Footnotes and references

1 From *Immacallam in dá Thúarad* from the Book of Leinster, cited in Meyer (1904), p. 185.

2 Meyer, Kuno (1881), *Revue Celtique,* Vol. V., p. 195. See also https://www.vanhamel.nl/codecs/Macgnímartha_Find (Extracted 1st April 2021).

3 Ibid.

4 See appendix 2. An embellished version of the tale is recounted by Doreen McBride in *Louth Folk Tales* (The History Press Ireland, 2015), which had been told to her by her great-grand-mother Martha Henry on Belfast's Shankill Road. O'Rahilly (1946), p. 330, suggests that the myth of the Salmon of Knowledge has been 'better preserved' in these oral versions.

5 Meyer (1904), pp. 185-6.

6 The poem in its entirety can be found in the appendix.

7 MacKillop (1998), p. 202.

8 Bondarenko (2012), p. 130.

9 Meyer (1904), p. 181.

10 'The plain of the Liffey, a very level plain in County Kildare,' O'Donovan, cited in Meyer (1904), p. 183.

11 Ibid., p. 183.

12 Ibid.

13 http://dil.ie/15213 (Extracted 5th April 2021).

14 http://dil.ie/15210 (Extracted 5th April 2021).

15 Meyer (1904), p. 187.

16 O'Rahilly (1946), p. 329 footnote 4, says that '*Finn Eces* is properly the name, not of Finn's tutor, but of Finn himself'.

17 MacKillop, op. cit., p. 120.

18 https://www.teanglann.ie/ga/fgb/giolla (Extracted 5th April 2021).

19 MacKillop, op. cit., p. 223.

20 Meyer, Kuno (1904), p.186.

21 Campbell (1988), p. 69.

22 Ibid., p. 71.

23 Ibid., p. 72.

24 Ibid.

25 Meyer (1904), pp. 182, 184, 185, etc.

26 Rees & Rees (1961), p. 249.

27 O'Rahilly (2006), pp. 140-142.

28 MacKillop (1998), pp. 102, 339.

29 O'Rahilly, op. cit., p. 142.

30 Ibid., pp. 136-7.

31 Rees & Rees (1961), p. 250.

32 Meyer (1904), p. 185.

33 Hogan (1910).

34 See https://www.dias.ie/celt/celt-publications-2/onomasticon-goedelicum/

35 Hogan, op. cit., p. 490.

36 Ibid.

37 Hickey (2000), pp. 65-8. See also Murphy, Anthony (2017), 'Cleitech, Rosnaree and the ancient ford of the Boyne' in *Mythical Ireland: New Light on the Ancient Past,* Liffey Press, pp. 176-181.

38 Murphy (2019), p. 167.

39 One of the best-known stories relating to Newgrange, *Altram Tige Dá Medar,* the Fosterage of the House of the Two Methers, mentions that, in apportioning the various *síd* mounds to the Dé Danann nobles, Sidh Cleitigh is assigned to 'Derg of swift eloquence'. See Duncan (1932), p. 207.

40 MD II, p. 10.

41 Holten (2016), p. 530.

42 Stout (2002), p. 141.

43 The two weirs are recorded in the Sites and Monuments Record and can be viewed (with detailed information) on the Historic Environment Viewer at https://maps.archaeology.ie/HistoricEnvironment/ The record numbers for the weirs are ME019-068002- and ME019-068003- (Extracted 5th April 2021).

44 Went, Arthur E.J., (1953) *Material for a history of the fisheries of the River Boyne,* County Louth Archaeological Journal XIII, 18-33, cited on https://maps.archaeology.ie/HistoricEnvironment/ (Extracted 5th April 2021).

45 See *'To the Journey's End: The Lifecycle of the Atlantic Salmon'* at https://youtu.be/65EfIjADGSc (Extracted 5th April 2021). For more about the salmon runs and their possible significance to Neolithic ceremonies at Newgrange, see Hensey (2015), pp. 79-84.

46 Stout, op. cit., pp. 89-91.

47 Went (1953), p. 23.

48 Ibid.

49 Stout (2002), p 86, fig. 4.

50 Went (1953), p. 23.

51 Borlase (1897), p. 346.

52 This is admittedly conjectural.

53 MacKillop, op. cit., p. 265. See also Hogan, op. cit., p. 490.

54 MD II, p. 11.

55 MacKillop, op. cit., p. 193.

56 See Anecdota IV for a version of the glossary edited from the Yellow Book of Lecan by Kuno Meyer.

57 https://www.teanglann.ie/ga/fgb/féach (Extracted 6th April 2021).

58 http://dil.ie/21449 (Extracted 6th April 2021).

59 Found at dil.ie. It is a digital dictionary of medieval Irish and is based on the Royal Irish Academy's Dictionary of the Irish language based mainly on Old and Middle Irish materials covering the period c.700 to c.1700 but incorporates corrections and additions to thousands of entries.

60 http://dil.ie/21457 (Extracted 6th April 2021).

61 O'Donovan & Stokes (1868), p.81.

62 Ibid.

63 dil.ie/21474 (Extracted 6th April 2021).

64 https://www.duchas.ie/en/cbes/5009003/4975847/5113488 (Extracted 6th April 2021).

65 Dooley & Roe (2008), pp. 4, 72.

66 AFM I, p.463.

67 Hennessy (1887), p. 347.

68 AC, pp. 138-9.

69 O'Donovan (1856), pp. 462-3.

70 I prefer Rosnaree (with one s) over Rossnaree, because the former is closer to the Irish.

71 The Irish place names website www.logainm.ie is an invaluable resource for tracking down information about Irish townland names. For Rossnaree, see: https://www.logainm.ie/38699.aspx (Extracted 6th April 2021).

72 Keating's account of the death and burial of Cormac Mac Airt is given in John O'Donovan's Ordnance Survey Letters for Meath. See OSL Meath, p. 76.

73 Hickey (2000), p. 59.

74 https://www.teanglann.ie/ga/fgb/ros (Extracted 6th April 2021).

75 O'Donovan & Stokes (1868), p. 141.

76 It should be pointed out here that there seems to be a lack of written evidence for the presence of salmon weirs on the Boyne before the time of the Cistercian arrival in the 12th century. In either case, the Pool of Ros is problematic at the time the annals say the Norsemen brought their ships upriver to Linn Rois. If there was a weir there, did the Vikings carry their boats over it, either across the weir or on the adjacent river bank? If there was no weir there, there is a diminished likelihood of the presence of a stagnant pool.

77 dil.ie/35551 (Extracted 6th April 2021).

78 ZCP, vol. XIX, p. 128, cited in http://dil.ie/35551.

79 http://dil.ie/35365 (Extracted 7th April 2021).

80 http://dil.ie/22221 (Extracted 7th April 2021).

81 Meyer (1904), p. 186.

82 Meyer (1881) RC V, p. 201.

83 Ibid., footnote 1, p. 186.

84 Ibid., p. 186.

85 dil.ie/40394 (Extracted 6th April 2021). *Filid* is a seer, diviner or a poet.

86 dil.ie/40403 (Extracted 6th April 2021). This is fascinating because the cracking open of the *cnó* (the hazel nuts on which the Salmon of Knowledge is said to have fed) is an image used repeatedly in my mytho-poetic work *Return to Segais*, which is inspired to a significant extent by the story of the Salmon of Knowledge and the Well of Segais. Much of *Return to Segais* was written spontaneously, as if illuminated

by some unknown source of inspiration. See Murphy (2021), pp. 32-35.

87 ZCP XVII, p. 156, cited in O'Rahilly (1946), p. 337.

88 O'Rahilly (1946), p. 322.

89 Ibid., pp. 322-3.

90 Ibid., p. 338.

91 Meyer (1904), p. 186, footnote 2.

92 O'Donovan & Stokes (1868), p. 94.

93 Ibid., pp.94-5.

94 One of the most widely-cited instances is the report by the Norman churchman and historian Giraldus Cambrensis (Gerald of Wales) about an inauguration rite in the far north of Ulster in which the one who would be king ritually mates with a white mare before the horse is killed, cut to pieces and boiled in water. The man bathes in the bloody water and imbibes some of the broth in order that his kingship be conferred. See O'Meara (1982), pp. 109-110.

95 MacKillop (1998), p. 58. The *tarbfes* is also mentioned in *Serglige Con Culainn*, 'The wasting sickness of Cú Chulainn' in Lebor na hUidre. The Irish text is in Best, R.I. and Bergin, Osborn (eds) (1929), *Lebor na hUidre: Book of the Dun Cow*, Royal Irish Academy, p. 109. An English translation by Eugene O'Curry runs thus: 'There was then prepared a bull-feast by them there, in order that they should discover out of it to whom they would give the sovereignty. Thus was that bull-feast prepared, namely : a white bull was killed, and one man eat enough of his flesh, and of his broth ; and he

slept under that meal ; and a charm of truth was pronounced on him by four Druids ; and he saw in a dream the shape of the man who should be made king there, and his form, and his description, and the sort of work that he was engaged in.' The O'Curry translation can be found in *The Sick-bed of Cuchulainn and the Only Jealousy of Eimer,* Atlantis 1 (1858) 362-369; 2 (1859) 98-124.

96 O'Rahilly (1946), p. 334.

97 Ibid., p. 335.

98 See Graves (1990), Vol. I., p.245, and Graves (1999), p. 224.

99 Curtin (1894), p. 474.

100 Meyer (1904), p. 186, footnote 3.

101 O'Donovan & Stokes (1868), p. 95.

102 http://dil.ie/16103 (Extracted 6th April 2021).

103 http://dil.ie/17282 (Extracted 6th April 2021).

104 Gwynn (1906), MD II, pp. 24-5.

105 Ibid., p. 25.

106 For more about the Mata and Lecc Benn, see Murphy (2017), pp. 57-65.

107 Gwynn, Lucius (1914), p. 230. I remember the first time I read that line. I punched the air with excitement. There was something in that claim about Dagda being the king of Linn Féic that enthralled me, and it was one of the inspiring factors that impelled me to do more research about the mysterious pool where the salmon was caught.

108 *Rí Indsi finni Fáil* (the king of the fair Isle of Fál), verse 56, from Gwynn, Lucius (1914), pp. 226, 234.

109 O'Donovan & Stokes (1868), pp. 144-5.

110 Ibid., p. 145.

111 Ibid., p. 145.

112 O'Rahilly (1946), p. 318.

113 Ibid.

114 Ibid., p. 319.

115 Macalister, LGE Part II., p. 195.

116 Anecdota, Vol. I, pp. 26-8. See also Bondarenko (2012), p. 141.

117 Hull, Eleanor, *The Colloquy between Fintan and the Hawk of Achill*, from Egerton 1782. https://sejh.pagesperso-orange.fr/keltia/version-en/fintan_achill.html (Extracted 7th April 2021).

118 O'Rahilly (1946), p. 319.

119 MacKillop (1998), p. 332. Rolleston (1910) says that 'this salmon was called Finntan in ancient times and was one of the Immortals, and he might be eaten and yet live'.

120 Gwynn (1903), p. 5.

121 Bondarenko (2012), p. 129.

122 Ibid., p. 130.

123 See LGE V, p. 113, where the relevant line from Amergin's chant is translated 'I am God who fashioneth Fire for a Head', with a note added, 'i.e. a giver of inspiration'.

124 dil.ie/22134 (Extracted 8th April 2021).

125 Bondarenko (2012), p.130.

126 Kalygin (2002), cited in Bondarenko (2012).

127 Bondarenko (2012), p. 130.

128 O'Rahilly, op. cit., p. 319. *In t-eó fis*, the Salmon of Wisdom, is mentioned in an obscure tale transcribed in ZCP viii, p. 227. Here is the Irish, with an English translation by American author Morgan Daimler, to whom I am grateful: *Ní thig dind aiream a scíath* (No high dwelling counting his wings) *Acht is failidh fiach da fáth* (But the Raven is cheerful (for) two reasons) *Muna ethaind in t-eó fis* (Unless he eats the salmon of knowledge) *Ní fetfaind beath ris co brath* (Not a smooth-feathered life exposed until Judgement day).

129 O'Rahilly (1946), p. 319.

130 https://sejh.pagesperso-orange.fr/keltia/version-en/fintan_achill.html, §21. (Extracted 7th April 2021).

131 O'Rahilly, op. cit., p. 319.

132 MD IV, pp.2-3.

133 O'Rahilly, op. cit., pp. 319-320.

134 Ibid.

135 MacKillop (1998), pp. 228-9.

136 Ibid., p. 228.

137 O'Rahilly, op. cit., p. 320.

138 Ibid. The anecdote can be found in Irish, transcribed by Kuno Meyer, in ZCP Vol. VIII (1912), p. 120.

139 O'Rahilly, op. cit., p. 320. The source of this account is Meyer, Kuno, *Anecdota from the Stowe Ms. No. 992*, in RC VI, p. 182.

140 O'Rahilly, op. cit., p. 320.

141 In *Tochmarc Étaín*, Elcmar resides at Cnuc Shide an Broga (Newgrange) and Echu Ollathir (Dagda), who in this tale resides at Uisnech Mide at the centre of Ireland, encourages his son, Óengus (Mac Óc) to take Newgrange from Elcmar. See Gantz (1981), pp. 39-42. In the short anecdote *De Gabáil int Síde* ('The Taking of the Otherworld Mound') found in the Book of Leinster, Dagda owns Newgrange and is tricked out of its possession by his son Oengus. See Murphy (2018), pp. 64-86. In *Altram Tighe Dá Mheadar*, Elcmar owns Síd in Broga and it is Manannán who encourages Óengus to shame Elcmar out of its ownership. See Duncan (1982).

142 Gantz (1981), p. 42.

143 Ó hÓgáin (1991), p. 326.

144 O'Grady (1892), Vol. II., p. 99.

145 MD III, p. 37.

146 Ó hÓgáin (1991), p. 326.

147 Ibid.

148 Ibid.

149 Ibid. Ó hÓgáin suggests that Finn/ Fionn/Find was a 'cult figure at the river Boyne from a quite archaic period' and that the lore of Nuadhu was introduced into the area in the last few centuries BC.

150 Ibid.

151 MacKillop (1998), p. 107.

152 O'Rahilly, op. cit., p. 321.

153 Ibid.

154 Rennes Dindshenchas, RC XV, pp. 440-1.

155 Ibid. The tale does not tell us any more about the identities of Ternóc's foster mother or Fursa, although MacKillop (1998), p. 216, says that Fursa is a name borne by numerous early Irish ecclesiastics.

156 Rennes Dindshenchas, RC XV, p. 441. There was a widespread belief a millennium ago that an Irish druid, Mog Ruith, had beheaded John the Baptist, and that at the time of the end of the world Ireland would be severely punished as a result.

157 O'Rahilly (1946), p. 333.

158 Ibid.

159 For more on the subject of saints restraining monsters, see 'Killing the monster', *infra*.

160 Ibid., p. 331.

161 MacCana (1973), p. 110.

162 Murphy and Moore (2020), p. 12.

163 Ó hÓgáin (1991), p.44

164 MacCana (1973), p. 110.

165 Ibid.

166 The location of the 'source' well varies. Rees & Rees (1961), p.161, say that: 'It is the source of the Boyne, the source of the Shannon, the source of the seven chief rivers of Ireland, and it has its counterpart in the Land of Promise

where the five rivers that flow from it are the five senses.'

167 Monaghan (2004), p. 50.

168 The principal sources for references to this great beast are in the Metrical and Prose Dindshenchas, where it is named, and also in *Tochmarc Emire,* The Wooing of Emer. For more about the Mata, see Murphy (2017), pp. 57-65.

169 RC XV, p.293. Tortoise is from the Irish *muir seilche* (lit. 'sea turtle' but *seilche* also means a snail or a monster, http://dil.ie/36903 (Extracted 7th April 2021). See also RC XI, p.434 (footnotes) by Kuno Meyer, where he relates, from Tochmarc Emire, '…a magic sea was on it, with a sea-turtle in it of a sucking nature, so that it would suck a man with his armour on to the ground of its…'.

170 RC XV, p. 293.

171 MD III, p. 101.

172 Ibid.

173 Ibid.

174 For more about the mysterious stone, Lecc Benn, upon which the monster was killed at Newgrange, see Murphy (2017), pp. 57-65.

175 MD II, p. 25.

176 Meyer (1888), p. 153.

177 MD II, p. 23.

178 MacKillop (1998), p. 312.

179 Ibid.

180 O'Rahilly (1946), pp. 333-4.

181 Prose Dindshenchas, RC XV p. 329.

182 See Murphy (2017), p. 58, and Freund (2003), Chapter 6: 'Out of the Monster'.

183 The story is recorded in the Schools Folklore Collection and can be read (as Gaeilge) online at https://www.duchas.ie/en/cbes/4493626/4405461 (Extracted 8th April 2021).

184 https://www.duchas.ie/en/cbes/4493626/4405501/4514292 (Extracted 8th April 2021).

185 LGE V pp. 57-9.

186 Ibid., pp. 110-111.

187 Ibid., p 59.

188 For a mytho-poetic exploration of Amergin's incantation, and indeed the journey of the Atlantic salmon in and out of the river Boyne, see Murphy (2021).

189 LGE V pp. 114-115. Murphy (2021), p. 165.

190 Jung (1990), pp. 17-18.

191 Ibid., p. 17.

192 Ibid., p. 18.

193 Ibid., p. 17.

194 Ibid., p. 18.

195 Ibid.

196 Ibid.

197 The well is 'symbolical of the unconscious', says Campbell (1988), p. 74.

198 One folk retelling of the story of the Salmon of Knowledge says that the

69

well over which the hazel trees grew was near the bridge at Slane – which is only two and a half miles 94km) upriver of Fiacc's Pool. See https://www.duchas. ie/en/cbes/5009003/4975847/5113488 (Extracted 8th April 2021). See appendix for the full story.

199 MD III, pp. 293-5. In this case, the well described is the source of the Shannon river, but the stories of the Boyne and Shannon are similar in many respects.

200 Jung, op. cit., p. 18.

201 Ibid., p. 19.

202 Ibid., p. 20.

203 MD III, p. 31.

204 Ibid.

205 Jung, op. cit., p. 20.

206 Ibid., p. 23.

207 Ibid., p. 21.

208 Ibid., p. 23.

209 Ibid., p. 24.

210 Ibid.

211 Campbell (1988), p. 173.

212 AFM I, pp. 115-117. For another summary of the death of Cormac, see OSL Meath, p. 76.

213 dil.ie/37359 (Extracted 8th April 2021)

214 AFM I, pp. 115-117.

215 AC, p. 60. There is also a reference to the death of Cormac, 'when the

salmon-bone stuck in his gullet' in MD IV, p. 203.

216 MD II, p. 15.

217 O'Grady (1892), Vol II., p. 97.

218 Rees & Rees (1961), p. 232.

219 AFM I, p. 121.

220 Ibid., p. 120.

221 Ibid.

222 MD II, p. 13.

223 Meyer, Kuno, *The Death of Finn Mac Cumaill,* in ZCP Vol I (1897), p. 462.

224 RC XVII (1896), p. 21.

225 *Teasmolad Corbmaic úi Cuinn ocus Finn meic Cumhaill sunn,* 'Here is the Panegyric of Conn's son Cormac and the Death of Finn son of Cumhaill', in O'Grady (1892), Vol II, pp. 96-99.

226 O'Grady (1892), Vol II, p. 98.

227 Meyer, Kuno, *The Death of Finn Mac Cumaill,* in ZCP Vol I (1897), p. 464.

228 Ibid., p. 463.

229 Ibid., p. 465.

230 Ibid., pp. 464-465.

231 Duncan (1932), p. 219.

232 Meyer (1904), p. 185.

233 Duncan (1932), p. 218.

234 Ibid., p. 219.

235 Ibid.

236 Dooley & Roe (2008), p.4.

237 MD IV p. 201.

238 Ibid.

239 Meyer (1904), pp. 186-187.

240 The Schools' Collection, Volume 0159, Page 135, by Dúchas © National Folklore Collection, UCD is licensed under CC BY-NC 4.0.

241 The Schools' Collection, Volume 0679, Page 129, by Dúchas © National Folklore Collection, UCD is licensed under CC BY-NC 4.0.

242 The Schools' Collection, Volume 0680, Page 041, by Dúchas © National Folklore Collection, UCD is licensed under CC BY-NC 4.0.

243 The Schools' Collection, Volume 0713, Page 139, by Dúchas © National Folklore Collection, UCD is licensed under CC BY-NC 4.0.

244 The Schools' Collection, Volume 0713, Page 149, by Dúchas © National Folklore Collection, UCD is licensed under CC BY-NC 4.0.

245 The Schools' Collection, Volume 0520, Page 384, by Dúchas © National Folklore Collection, UCD is licensed under CC BY-NC 4.0.

246 The Schools' Collection, Volume 0597, Page 166, by Dúchas © National Folklore Collection, UCD is licensed under CC BY-NC 4.0.